LITTLE
SCOTTISH
SONGBOOK

ILLUSTRATED BY
CLARE HEWITT

Appletree Press

First published in 1994 by
The Appletree Press Ltd
19–21 Alfred Street
Belfast BT2 8DL

Copyright © The Appletree Press Ltd 1994

Typeset by Seton Music Graphics Ltd.
Printed in the EC.

A catalogue record for this book is
available from the British Library.

ISBN 0-86281-482-0

9 8 7 6 5 4 3 2 1

Contents

Loch Lomond

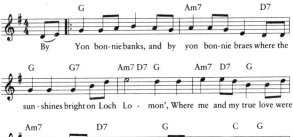

By Yon bon-nie banks, and by yon bon-nie braes where the sun-shines bright on Loch Lo - mon', Where me and my true love were e - ver wont to gae, On the bon-nie, bon-nie banks o' Loch Lo - mon'.

Chorus:

Oh You tak' the high road, and

I'll tak' the low road An' I'll be in Scot-land a-
fore ye, But me and my true love will
nev-er meet a-gain On the bon-nie, bon-nie banks o' Loch
Lo - mon' Twas___ Lo - mon'.

There that we parted in yon shady glen.
On the steep, steep side of Ben Lomon',
Where in purple hue, the hielan' hills we view,
An' the moon comin' out in the gloamin'.

Chorus

The wee birdies sing, and the wild flowers spring,
While in sunshine the waters are sleepin'
But the broken heart it kens nae second spring again,
Tho' the waefu' may cease frae their greetin'.

Chorus

Bonnie Dundee

Capo 2nd

To the Lords of Con-ven-tion 'twas Cla-ver house spoke, Ere the
King's crown go down there are crowns to be broke, So
each cav-a-lier who loves hon-our and me Let him
fol-low the bon-nets o' Bon-nie Dun-dee. *Chorus:* Come

fill up my cup, come fill up my can, Come sad-dle my hor-ses and call up my men, Un-hook the West Port __ and let us gae free, For it's up with the bon-nets o' Bon-nie Dun-dee.

Dundee he is mounted, he rides up the street,
The bells are rung backward, the drums they are beat;
But the Provost, douce man, says "Just e'en let him be,"
The toun is weel quit of that deil o' Dundee.

Chorus

There are hills ayont Pentland, and lands ayont Forth,
If there's Lords in the south there are Chiefs in the north;
There are brave dhunie wassals three thousand times three,
Will cry "Hey for the Bonnets o' Bonnie Dundee!"

Come fill up my cup, come fill up my can,
Come saddle my horses and call up my men,
Unhook the West Port and let me gae free,
And it's room for the Bonnets of Bonnie Dundee

Awa' to the hills, to the woods, to the rocks,
Ere I own a usurper, I'll couch with the fox;
And tremble, false Whigs, in the midst o' your glee,
You've no' seen the last o' my Bonnets and me!

Come fill up my cup, come fill up my can,
Come saddle my horses and call up my men,
Fling all your gates open, and let me gae free,
For it's up with the Bonnets of Bonnie Dundee.

Caller Herrin'

Wha'll buy cal - ler her - rin? They're bon - nie fish and hale-some fa - rin',

Wha'll buy cal - ler her - rin', New drawn frae the Forth? When

ye were sleep -in' on your pil - lows, Dream'd ye ought o' our puir fel - lows,

Dark - ling as they fac'd the bil - lows, A' to fill the wo-ven wil - lows,

Buy my caller herrin', New drawn frae the Forth. Wha'll
buy my caller herrin? They're no brought here without brave daring;
Buy my caller herrin' Hauld thro' wind and rain. Wha'll
buy my caller herrin? Oh ye may ca' them vulgar farin',
Wives and mithers maist despairing
Ca' them lives o' men. Ca' them lives o' men.

And when the creel o' herrin' passes,
Ladies, clad in silks and laces,
Gather in their braw pelisses,
Cast their heads and screw their faces.
Buy my caller herrin'
New drawn frae the Forth.

Chorus

10

Gude caller herrin's no got lightlie,
Ye can trip the spring fu' tightlie,
Spite o' tauntin', flauntin', flingin',
Gow has set you a' a-singin'.
Buy my caller herrin'
New drawn frae the Forth.

Chorus

But neebour wives, now tent my tellin',
When the bonny fish ye're sellin',
At ae word be in ye're dealin'__
Truth will stand when a' thing's failin'.
Buy my caller herrin'
New drawn frae the Forth.

Chorus

Charlie Is My Darling

Chorus: Oh! Char-lie is my dar-ling, My dar-ling, my dar-ling, Oh!

Char-lie is my dar-ling, The young Che-va-lier. 'Twas

on a Mon-day morn-ing, Right ear-ly in the year, That

Char-lie came to our town, The young Che-va-lier. Oh!

Char - lie is my dar - ling, My dar - ling, my dar - ling; Oh!
Char - lie is my dar - ling, The young Che - va-lier.

As he came marching up the street,
The pipes play'd loud and clear,
and a' the folk came rinnin' out
To meet the Chevalier.

Chorus

Wi' hieland bonnets on their heads,
And claymores bright and clear,
They came to fight for Scotland's right,
And the young Chevalier.

Chorus

They've left their bonny hieland hills,
Their wives and bairnies dear,
To draw the sword for Scotland's lord,
The young Chevalier.

Chorus

Oh there were mony beating hearts,
And mony hopes and fears;
And mony were the prayers put up
For the young Chevalier.

Chorus

13

Ye Banks and Braes

Ye banks and braes o' bonnie Doon, How can ye bloom sae fresh and fair? How can ye chant, ye little birds, And I sae weary, fu' of care! Thou'lt

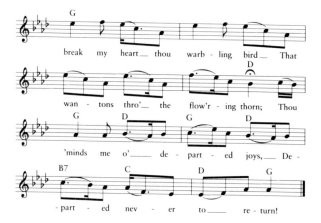

break my heart_ thou warb - ling bird_ That
wan - tons thro'_ the flow'r - ing thorn; Thou
'minds me o'_ de - part - ed joys, _ De -
- part - ed nev - er to _ re - turn!

Oft have I rov'd by bonnie Doon,
To see the rose and woodbine twine;
And ilka bird sang o' its love,
And fondly sae did I o' mine.
Wi' lightsome heart I pu'd a rose,
Fu' sweet upon its thorny tree:
And my fause lover stole my rose,
But Ah! he left the thorn wi' me!

The Flowers of the Forest

Capo 1st

I've seen the smi - ling of For - tune be - guil - ing, I've
tast - ed her fa - vours and felt her de - cay:
Sweet was her bless - ing and kind her ca - ress - ing, But
now they are fled fled far a - way.

I've seen the for - est a - dorn'd the fore - most Wi' flowers o' the fair - est baith pleas - ant and gay, Sae bon - nie was their bloom - ing, their scent the air per - fu - ming, But now they are with - er'd and a' wede a - way.

I've seen the morning wi' gold the hills adorning,
And loud tempests roaring before parting day,
I've seen Tweed's silver streams, glitt'ring in the sunny beams,
Grow drumlie and dark as they roll'd on their way.
O fickle Fortune why this cruel sporting?
Why thus perplex us poor sons of a day?
Thy frown cannot fear me, thy smile cannot cheer me;
Since the flowers o' the forest are a' wede away.

Mary of Argyle

I have heard the ma-vis sing-ing His love song to the morn; I have seen the dew-drop cling-ing To the rose just new-ly born: But a sweet-er song has cheer'd me, At the ev'-ning's gen-tle close; And I've seen an eye still bright-er Than the dew-drop on the rose. 'Twas thy

voice my gen-tle Ma-ry, And thine art-less win-ning smile, That made this world an E - den Bon-ny Ma-ry of Ar-gyle.

Tho' thy voice may lose its sweetness,
And thine eye its brightness too;
Tho' thy step may lack its fleetness,
And thy hair its sunny hue;
Still to me wilt thou be dearer
Than all the world shall own.
I have lov'd thee for thy beauty
But not for that alone.
I have watch'd thy heart, dear Mary,
And its goodness was the wile,
That has made thee mine for ever
Bonny Mary of Argyle.

The Blue Bell of Scotland

The Rose sum-mer's em-blem 'tis Eng-land's cho-sen tree, And France decks her shield with the state-ly Fleur-de-lis. But bright-er, fair-er far than those, There blooms a flow'r for me, 'Tis the Blue bell, the Blue bell On Scot-land's grass-y lea. Where

from the dark, up-springs the lark The ris-ing sun to see! Where

from the dark up-springs the lark, The ris-ing sun to see!

My land! native land!
Where afar my steps have been,
Blue skies charm the eyes,
And the earth is ever green.
Yet dwelt my heart 'mid Scotland's glens,
Where aye in thought was seen,
The Blue bell, the Blue bell,
Amid the bracken green,
And brighter far than sun or star,
The eyes of bonnie Jean!
And brighter far than sun or star,
The eyes of bonnie Jean!

The Thistle, Scotland's badge
Up from Freedom's soil it grew,
Her foes aye found it hedg'd round
With rosemarie and rue.
And, emblem that her daughters were modest, leal, and true,
From off the rocks, to deck their locks,
They pluck'd the Bell of Blue!
The Heathbell, the Harebell,
Old Scotland's Bell of Blue!
The Heathbell, the Harebell,
Old Scotland's Bell of Blue.

Annie Laurie

Max - well -ton braes are bon - nie, Where ear - ly fa's the dew, And it's there that An - nie Lau - rie Gie'd me _ her pro - mise true; Gie'd me her pro - mise true, Which ne'er for - got will be; And for bon - nie An - nie

Lau - rie I'd____ lay_ me doun and dee.

Her brow is like the snaw-drift,
Her neck is like the swan;
Her face it is the fairest
That e'er the sun shone on.
That e'er the sun shone on,
And dark blue is her e'e;
And for bonnie Annie Laurie
I'd lay me doun and dee.

Like dew on the gowan lying,
Is the fa' o' her fairy feet;
And like winds in summer sighing,
Her voice is low and sweet.
Her voice is low and sweet,
And she is a' the world to me
And for bonnie Annie Laurie
I'd lay me doun and dee.

Fair Helen of Kirkconnell

I wish I were where Hel-en lies, For night and day on me she cries; For night and day on me she cries, I wish I were where Hel-en lies On fair Kirk-con-nell lea. Oh Hel-en fair! oh

Hel-en chaste! Were I with thee I ___ would be blest, Were
I with thee I ___ would be blest, Where thou liest low and
at thy rest On ___ fair Kirk-con-nell ___ lea. ___

Oh Helen fair beyond compare,
I'll make a garland of thy hair,
I'll make a garland of thy hair
Shall bind my heart for ever mair,
Until the day I die.
Curs'd be the heart that hatch'd the thought,
And curs'd the hand that fir'd the shot,
And curs'd the hand that fir'd the shot,
When in my arms dear Helen dropt
And died to succour me.

O think na but my heart was sair,
My love dropt down and spak nae mair!
My love dropt down and spak nae mair!
O think na ye my heart was sair
On fair Kirkconnell lea!
Where Helen lies, where Helen lies!
I wish I were where Helen lies!
I wish I were where Helen lies!
Soon may I be where Helen lies!
Who died for love of me!

I Lo'e Na A Laddie But Ane

I lo'e na a lad-die but ane, ___ He lo'es na a las-sie but me; ___ He's wil-lin' to make me his ain, And his ain I am wil-lin' to be. ___ He coft me a rok-ley o' blue ___ And a pair o' mit-tens sae

green; ___ He vow'd that he'd ev-er be true, ___ And I
plight - ed my troth ___ yes - treen. ___

Let ithers brag weel o' their gear,
Their land and their lordly degree,
I care na for ought but my dear,
For he's ilka thing lordly to me.
His words mair than sugar are sweet,
His sense drives ilk fear far awa;
I listen, poor fool, and I greet;
Yet how sweet are the tears as they fa'.

"Dear lassie," he cries wi' a jeer,
"Ne'er heed what the auld anes will say;
Tho' we've little to brag o', ne'er fear,
What's gowd to a heart that is wae?
Our laird has baith honours and wealth,
Yet see how he's dwining wi' care;
Now we, tho' we've naething but health,
Are canty and leal ever mair."

"O Menie! the heart that is true,
Has something mair precious than gear;
Ilk ev'n it has naething to rue,
Ilk morn it has naething to fear.
Ye warldlings gae hoard up your store,
And tremble for fear ought ye tyne;
Guard your treasure with lock, bar and door,
True love is the guardian o' mine."

My Love Is Like A Red, Red Rose

O my love is like a red, red, rose, That's new-ly sprung in June! O my

love is like a me-lo-die That's sweet-ly play'd in tune   As

fair art thou my bon-nie lass, So   deep in love am I: And

I will love thee still my dear, Till   a' the seas gang dry.   Till

a' the seas gang dry, my dear, Till a' the seas gang dry, And

I will love thee still, my dear, Till a' the seas gang dry.

Till a' the seas gang dry, my dear,
And the rocks melt wi' the sun;
And I will love thee still, my dear,
While the sands of life shall run.
But, fare thee weel, my only love!
O fare thee weel awhile!
And I will come again, my love,
Tho' 'twere ten thousand mile.
Tho' 'twere ten thousand mile, my love,
Tho' 'twere ten thousand mile;
And I will come again, my love,
Tho' 'twere ten thousand mile.

When The Kye Come Hame

Come all ye jol-ly shep-herds that whis-tle through the glen, I'll

tell ye of a se-cret That cour-tiers din-na ken: What

is the great-est bliss That the tongue o' man can name? 'Tis to

woo a bon-nie las-sie When the kye come hame. When the

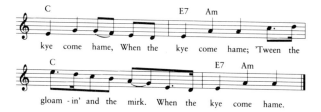

kye come hame, When the kye come hame; 'Tween the
gloam - in' and the mirk. When the kye come hame.

'Tis not beneath the burgonet
Nor yet beneath the crown,
'Tis not on couch of velvet
Nor yet on bed of down
'Tis beneath the spreading birch,
In the dell without a name,
Wi' a bonnie bonnie lassie
When the kye come hame.

Chorus

Then the eye shines sae bright
The haill saul to beguile,
There's love in every whisper,
And joy in every smile;
O who would choose a crown,
Wi' its perils and its fame,
And miss a bonnie lassie
When the kye come hame.

Chorus

See yonder pawky shepherd
That lingers on the hill
His yowes are in the fauld
And his lambs are lying still
Yet he downa gang to rest
For his heart is in a flame
To meet his bonnie lassie
When the kye come hame.

Chorus

Awa' wi' fame and fortune
What comfort can they gie?
And a' the arts that prey upon
Man's life and liberty!
Gie me the highest joy
That the heart o' man can frame,
My bonnie, bonnie lassie
When the kye come hame.

Chorus

Wae's Me For Prince Charlie

A wee_ bird_ cam to our_ ha'_ door, He
war-bled_ sweet and_ clear-lie, And aye_ the_ o'er come
o'_ his_ sang Was "Wae's me_ for Prince Char-lie. Oh
when_ I_ heard the bon-nie, bon-nie bird, The

tears came drap-pin' rare - ly; I took_my_bon-net aff_ my head For weel I_ lo'ed Prince Char - lie.

Quo' I my bird, my bonnie, bonnie bird,
Is that a sang ye borrow?
Are these some words ye've learn't by heart?
Or a lilt o' dool and sorrow?
"Oh no, no, no," the wee bird sang,
"I've flown sin' mornin' early,
But sic a day o' wind and rain:
Oh wae's me for Prince Charlie!

"On hills that are by right his ain,
He roams a lonely stranger;
On ilka hand he's press'd by want,
On ilka side is danger.
Yestreen I met him in a glen,
My heart maist bursted fairly,
For sadly chang'd indeed was he:
Oh wae's me for Prince Charlie!"

"Dark night cam' on, the tempest howl'd
Loud owre the hills and valleys;
And whar was't that your Prince lay down,
Wha's hame should been a palace?
He row'd him in a Highland plaid,
Which cover'd him but sparely,
And slept beneath a bush o' broom;
Oh wae's me for Prince Charlie!"

But now the bird saw some red-coats,
And he shook his wings wi' anger:
"Oh this is no a land for me,
I'll tarry here nae langer."
A while he hover'd on the wing,
Ere he departed fairly;
But weel I mind the fareweel strain,
'Twas— "Wae's me for Prince Charlie!"

Jock O'Hazeldean

"Why weep ye by the tide, la-dye, Why weep ye by the

tide?____ I'll wed ye to my young-est son, And

ye shall be his bride; And ye shall be his

bride, la-dye, Sae come-ly to_ be seen:" But

aye she loot the tears down fa, For Jock o' Ha - zel - dean.

Now let this wilful grief be done,
And dry that cheek so pale;
Young Frank is chief of Errington,
And lord of Langley dale:
His step is first in peacefu' ha',
His sword in battle keen,
But aye she loot the tears down fa',
For Jock o' Hazeldean.

A chain of gowd ye shall not lack,
Nor braid to bind your hair,
Nor mettled hound, nor managed hawk,
Nor palfrey fresh and fair;
And you, the foremost o' them a'
Shall ride our forest queen,
But aye she loot the tears down fa',
For Jock o' Hazeldean.

The kirk was decked at morning-tide,
The tapers glimmer'd fair;
The priest and bridegroom wait the bride,
But ne'er a bride was there.
They sought her baith by bower and ha',
The ladye was na seen,
She's owre the border and awa
Wi' Jock o' Hazeldean.

The Rowan Tree

Oh!___ Row - an Tree, Oh! Row - an Tree! thou'lt
aye be dear to me,___ En - twin'd thou art wi' mo - ny ties, o'
hame and in - fan - cy. Thy leaves were aye the first o' spring, Thy
flow'rs the sim - mer's pride; There was nae sic a bonny tree in

a' the coun-trie side.   Oh!   Row - an tree.

How fair wert thou in simmer time, wi' a' thy clusters white,
How rich and gay thy autumn dress, wi' berries red and bright.
On thy fair stem were many names, which now nae mair I see,
But they're engraven on my heart. Forgot they ne'er can be!
Oh! Rowan tree!

We sat aneath thy spreading shade, the bairnies round thee ran,
They pu'd thy bonny berries red, and necklaces they strang.
My Mother! Oh, I see her still, she smil'd oor sports to see,
Wi' little Jeanie on her lap, and Jamie at her knee!
Oh! Rowan tree!

Oh! there arose my Father's prayer, in holy evening's calm,
How sweet was then my Mother's voice, in the Martyr's psalm;
Now a' are gane! we meet nae mair aneath the Rowan Tree;
But hallowed thoughts around thee twine o' hame and infancy
Oh! Rowan tree!

A Hieland Lad

A— Hie-land lad my— love was born, The Law-land laws he— held in scorn;But he still was faith fu'— to his clan My— gal-lant braw John Hie-land man. Sing

Chorus:

hey! my braw John Hie-land man! Sing ho! my braw John

Hie-land man! There's no' a lad_ in_ a' the lan' Was
match_ for_ my_ John_ Hie - land man!

With his philabeg and tartan plaid,
And gude claymore down by his side;
The ladies' hearts he did trepan—
My gallant braw John Hielandman!

Chorus

They banish'd him beyond the sea,
But ere the bud was on the tree,
Adown my cheek the pearlies ran,
Embracing my John Hielandman.

Chorus

But oh, they caught him at the last
And bound him in a dungeon fast.
My curse upon them every wan—
They've hanged my braw John Hielandman!

Chorus

Skye Boat Song

Chorus: G

Speed bon - nie boat   like a   bird   on the wing,

G   C   G

"On-ward!" the sai - lors cry;   Car - ry the lad   that's

D7   G   C   G | Last time

born to be king   o - ver the sea   to   Skye. ___

Em   Am

Loud   the   winds howl,   loud   the   waves roar,

Thun-der-claps rend the air; Baff-led our foes stand by the shore, Fol-low they will not dare.

Chorus

Though the waves leap, soft shall ye sleep,
Ocean's a royal bed.
Rocked in the deep, Flora will keep
Watch by your weary head.

Chorus

Many's the lad fought on that day
Well the claymore could wield,
When the night came, silently lay
Dead on Culloden's field.

Chorus

Burned are our homes, exile and death
Scatter the loyal men;
Yet ere the sword cool in the sheath
Charlie will come again.

My Ain Kind Dearie

When o'er the hill the east - ern star Tells

bught in' time _ is _ near, my jo, And _

ow - sen frae the fur - row'd field Re -

- turn sae dowf _ and _ wear - ie O; Down

by — the burn, where scent - ed birks Wi'
dew— are — hang - ing clear, my jo, I'll —
meet thee on the lea - rig My ain — kind — dear-ie, O.

In mirkest glen at midnight hour
I'd rove and ne'er be eerie O,
If thro' that glen I gaed to thee
My ain kind dearie, O!
Altho' the night were ne'er sae wild,
And I were ne'er saé wearie, O,
I'd meet thee on the learig,
My ain kind dearie, O!

The hunter lo'es the morning sun,
To rouse the mountain deer, my jo,
At noon the fisher seeks the glen
Along the burn to steer my jo.
Gie me the hour o' gloamin' grey,
It maks my heart sae cheeie O,
To meet thee on the learig,
My ain kind dearie, O!

My Love She's But A Lassie Yet

Capo 1st

My love she's but a lass-ie yet. A— light-some love-ly las-sie yet; It— scarce wad do to sit an' woo Down by the stream sae glas-sy yet But— there's a braw time com-ing yet When we may gang a - roam-ing yet. An'— taste the bliss Of

love's first kiss,   When fa's_ the_ mo-dest   gloam-ing yet.

She's neither proud nor saucy yet,
She's neither plump nor gaucy yet;
But just a jinking,
Bonnie blinking,
Hilty skilty lassie yet.
But oh! her artless smile's mair sweet
Than hinny or than marmalete;
An' right or wrang,
Ere it be lang
I'll bring her to a parley yet.

I'm jealous o' what blesses her,
The very breeze that kisses her;
The flow'ry beds
On which she treads,
Though wae for ane that misses her.
Then oh! to meet my lassie yet,
Up in yon glen sae grassy yet;
For all I see
Are nought to me,
Save her that's but a lassie yet.

Bonnie Wee Thing

Bon - nie__ wee__ thing, can - ty__ wee thing,

Love - ly__ wee__ thing, wert thou__ mine;

I__ would wear__ thee in__ my__ bo - som,

Lest__ my__ jew - el I should__ tine.

Wist - ful - ly__ I __ look __ and __ lan - guish,
In that bon - nie__ face of __ thine; __
And my heart it stounds with an - guish,
Lest __ my__ wee__ thing be na__ mine.

Bonnie wee thing, canty wee thing,
Lovely wee thing, wert thou mine;
I would wear thee in my bosom,
Lest my jewel I should tine.
Wit and grace, and love, and beauty,
In ae constellation shine!
To adore thee is my duty,
Goddess o' this soul o' mine.

Auld Lang Syne

Should auld ac-quaint-ance be for-got, And nev-er brought to mind; Should auld ac-quaint-ance be for-got, And days o' lang ___ syne

Chorus:

For auld ___ lang - syne, my dear, For auld lang - syne; We'll

tak   a cup o'   kind-ness yet, For   auld _   lang - syne.

We twa hae run about the braes,
And pu'd the gowans fine,
But we've wander'd mony a weary foot,
Sin auld lang syne.

Chorus

We twa hae paidl't i' the burn,
Frae mornin' sun till dine:
But seas between us braid hae roar'd
Sin' auld lang syne.

Chorus

And here's a hand my trusty frien'
And gie's a hand o' thine;
And we'll tak a right guid willie-waught,
For auld lang syne.

Chorus

And surely ye'll be your pint stoup,
And surely I'll be mine;
And we'll tak a cup o' kindness yet,
For auld lang syne.

Chorus

51

Ca' The Yowes To The Knowes

Ca' the yowes to the knowes, Ca' them whar the heath-er grows,

Ca' them whar the burn-ie rowes, My bon-nie dear - ie. As

I gaed down the wa-ter side, There I met my shep-herd lad, He

row'd me sweet-ly in his plaid, And ca'd me his dear - ie.

Ca' the yowes to the knowes,
Ca' them whar the heather grows;
Ca' them whar the burnie rows,
My bonnie dearie.
Will ye gang down the water side,
And see the waves sae sweetly glide?
Beneath the hazels spreading wide,
The moon it shines fu' clearly.

Ca' the yowes to the knowes,
Ca' them whar the heather grows;
Ca' them whar the burnie rows,
My bonnie dearie.
While waters wimple to the sea;
While day blinks in the lift sae hie;
Till clay cauld death shall blin' my e'e,
Oh Ye shall be my dearie.

Come O'er The Stream Charlie

Capo 1st

Come o'er the stream, Char-lie, dear Char-lie, brave Char-lie, Come o'er the stream, Char-lie, and dine wi'Mac-Lean; And though you be wea-ry we'll make your heart cheer-y, And wel-come our Char-lie, and his loy-al

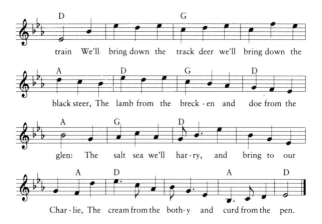

train We'll bring down the track deer we'll bring down the black steer, The lamb from the breck - en and doe from the glen: The salt sea we'll har - ry, and bring to our Char - lie, The cream from the both-y and curd from the pen.

And you shall drink freely the dews of Glen Sheerly
That stream in the starlight when kings dinna ken;
And deep be your meed of the wine that is red.
To drink to your sire and his friend the MacLean.

If aught will invite you, or more will delight you,
'Tis ready a troop of our bold Highland men
Shall range on the heather with bonnet and feather,
Strong arms and broad claymores, three hundred and ten.

The Four Maries

Yes-treen the Queen had four Ma-ries, The nicht she'll ha'e but three; There was Ma-rie Sea-ton, and Ma-rie Bea-ton, And Ma-rie Car-mi-chael and me. Oh oft-en ha'e I dress'd my Queen, And deck'd wi' gowd her hair, And

she has gien me in re-turn A hem-pen scarf to wear.

I ha'e but just begun to live,
And yet this day I dee;
Oh tie a napkin owre my face,
That the gallows I mayna' see!
My father kiss'd me and little thought,
When last he look'd on me,
That I his last and bonniest wean
Should hang on a gallows tree.

O little did my mother ken
The day she gied me breath,
That I should come sae far frae hame
For siccan a shamefu' death.
Ye mariners! Ye mariners!
That gang out owre the sea,
Let neither my father nor mother ken
What death I am to dee.

I charge ye a' ye mariners,
When ye sail owre the faem,
Let neither my father nor mither get wit
But that I'm coming hame;
For if my father and mither got wit,
And my bold brethren three,
O mickle wad be the guid red bluid
That day wad be spilt for me.

Blue Bonnets Over The Border

(Chorus:) G   C   G   C   G

March!   March!   Et - trick and Te - vi - ot - dale!
2. Come from the hills where the hir - sels are gra - zing,

C   G   C   G   D7   G

Why, my lads, din-na ye march for-ward in or - der?
come from the glen of the buck and the Roe____

G   C   G   D7   G

March!   March!   Esk - dale and Lid - des - dale,
Come to the Crag where the bea - con is blaz - ing,

All the Blue Bon-nets are o - ver the bor - der!
Come with the Buck-ler the lance and the bow____

1. Ma - ny a Ban - ner spread, Flut - ters a - bove your head,
Trum - pets are sound - ing, war steeds are bound - ing,

Ma - ny a crest that is fa - mous in sto - ry!
Stand to your arms___ and march in good or - der,

Mount and make rea - dy then, Sons of the moun - tain glen,
Eng - land shall ma-ny a day, talk of the bloo - dy fray

Fight for your King, and the old Scot-tish glo - ry.
When the Blue Bon - nets came o - ver the bor - der!

59

Chorus:

March! March! Et - trick and Te - vi - ot - dale,

Why my lads din - na, ye march for - ward in or - der?

March! March! Esk - dale and Lid - des - dale!

All the Blue Bon - nets are o - ver the bor - der!